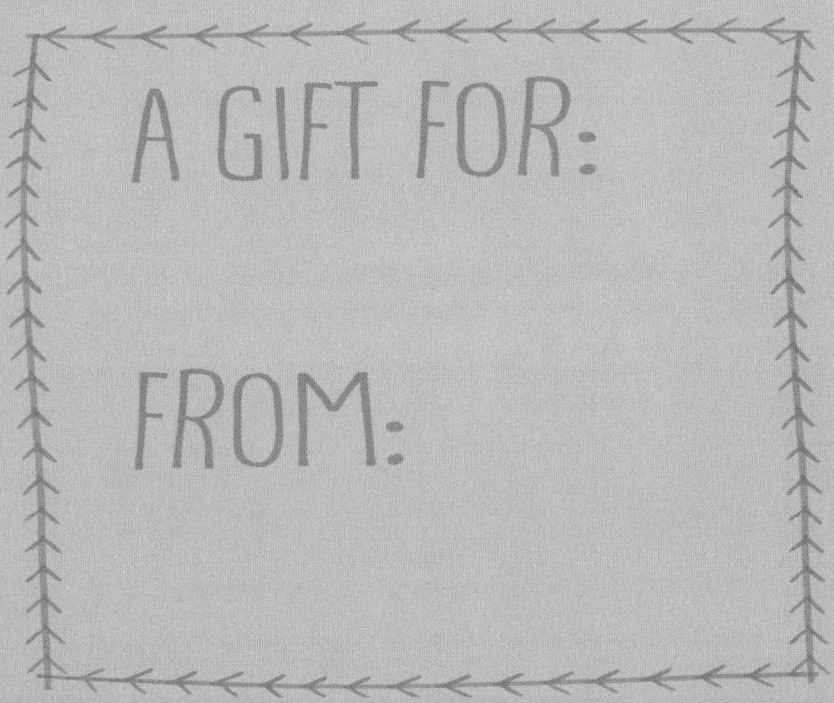

Wit & Wisdom of the Kitchen
Copyright © 2016 by Appleseed Press Book Publishers

This is an officially licensed book by Cider Mill Press Book Publishers LLC.

This edition published in 2016 by Hallmark Gift Books, a division of Hallmark Cards, Inc., Kansas City, MO 64141 under license from Cider Mill Press.

Visit us on the Web at Hallmark.com.

All rights reserved under the Pan-American and International Copyright Conventions.

No part of this book may be reproduced in whole or in part, scanned, photocopied, recorded, distributed in any printed or electronic form, or reproduced in any manner whatsoever, or by any information storage and retrieval system now known or hereafter invented, without express written permission of the publisher, except in the case of brief quotations embodied in critical articles and reviews.

The scanning, uploading, and distribution of this book via the Internet or via any other means without permission of the publisher is illegal and punishable by law. Please support authors' rights, and do not participate in or encourage piracy of copyrighted materials.

Cover design by Mark Voss Design
Interior design by Mark Voss Design

Photo Credits: All images and photographs are used under official license from Shutterstock.com

The quotation from Guy Fieri is from p.1 [introduction] from GUY FIERI FOOD by GUY FIERI with ANN VOLKWEIN. Copyright (c) 2011 by Guy Fieri. Reprinted with permission of HarperCollins Publishers.

The three quotations from Julia Child are provided courtesy of The Julia Child Foundation. The first and third quotes (in order of appearance) are excerpted from *My Life in France*, and the second quote is from The Biography Channel, Backstage with Julia, Culinary Institute LeNotre.

ISBN: 978-1-63059-916-4
BOK2282

Made in China
MAY16

WIT & WISDOM OF THE KITCHEN

Featuring a Lifetime of Cooking Knowledge Passed Down from Generations of Food Lovers

Dominique DeVito

Kennebunkport, Maine

Introduction

The kitchen is the heart of any home. It is where people come together to nurture and sustain themselves and others. It is where memories of all kinds are made, whether they are of the smell of fresh-made coffee, the sight of rolling out dough, the feel of the skin of an orange being peeled away, or the taste of sausage-infused spaghetti sauce—or the voices of your family, friends, and relatives as meals are prepared. The kitchen is a source for all the senses to be reawakened every day, at multiple times of the day.

Every cook has a collection of books that they turn to over and over for the kind of "wisdom" you'll find in the first section of this book, "Wit & Wisdom from the Experts." I grew up with some classics, including: *The Betty Crocker Illustrated Cookbook, The Joy of Cooking* by Irma Rombauer, *The Martha Stewart Living Cookbook,* James Beard's *Theory and Practice of Good Cooking* and his amazing book, *Beard on Bread*. I have subscribed to cooking magazines since I was a teenager. The wit and wisdom from the culinary experts is collected at the beginning of this book and will ring true to anyone who enjoys spending time cooking and eating. (Okay, that's practically everyone!)

Once you've been inspired, you will find a collection of my own cooking quips and tips, as well as a selection of recipes that come from my own time spent in the heart of the home: the kitchen. The "wisdom" I share in this section is from memories made, recipes tested, and conversations engaged in in the kitchens of my life, from my childhood home in Pennsylvania to the apartments I rented in my early adulthood to the houses I've called home with my family in New Jersey and New York. Kitchens, like life, provide wisdom in the forms of laughter, joy, celebration, frustration, disappointment, and tears. I know I've been blessed to experience them all and am thankful for each day and each meal and each gathering that continues to come from kitchens. The recipes featured in this second section, lovingly titled "From My Kitchen, to Yours," are guaranteed to please and should be staples at gatherings of family and friends—recipes for macaroni and cheese, fried chicken, the perfect apple pie, succulent meatloaf, chocolate chip cookies, and more. Sprinkled throughout are some technique tips and tricks for making these delicious dishes.

This book is a celebration of all of those ways the kitchen permeates our lives. In the end, though, it's getting into the kitchen and cooking where the magic happens and the wisdom comes alive. May your time in the kitchen yield great food and great memories.

Dominique DeVito

WIT & WISDOM
FROM THE EXPERTS

Kitchen wisdom
comes from many sources,
from your own friends and family
to beloved writers and celebrated chefs.
Enjoy this collection of my favorite
words of wisdom from the greats!

"One of the secrets, and pleasures, of cooking is to learn to correct something if it goes awry; and one of the lessons is to grin and bear it if it cannot be fixed."

JULIA CHILD, *My Life in France*

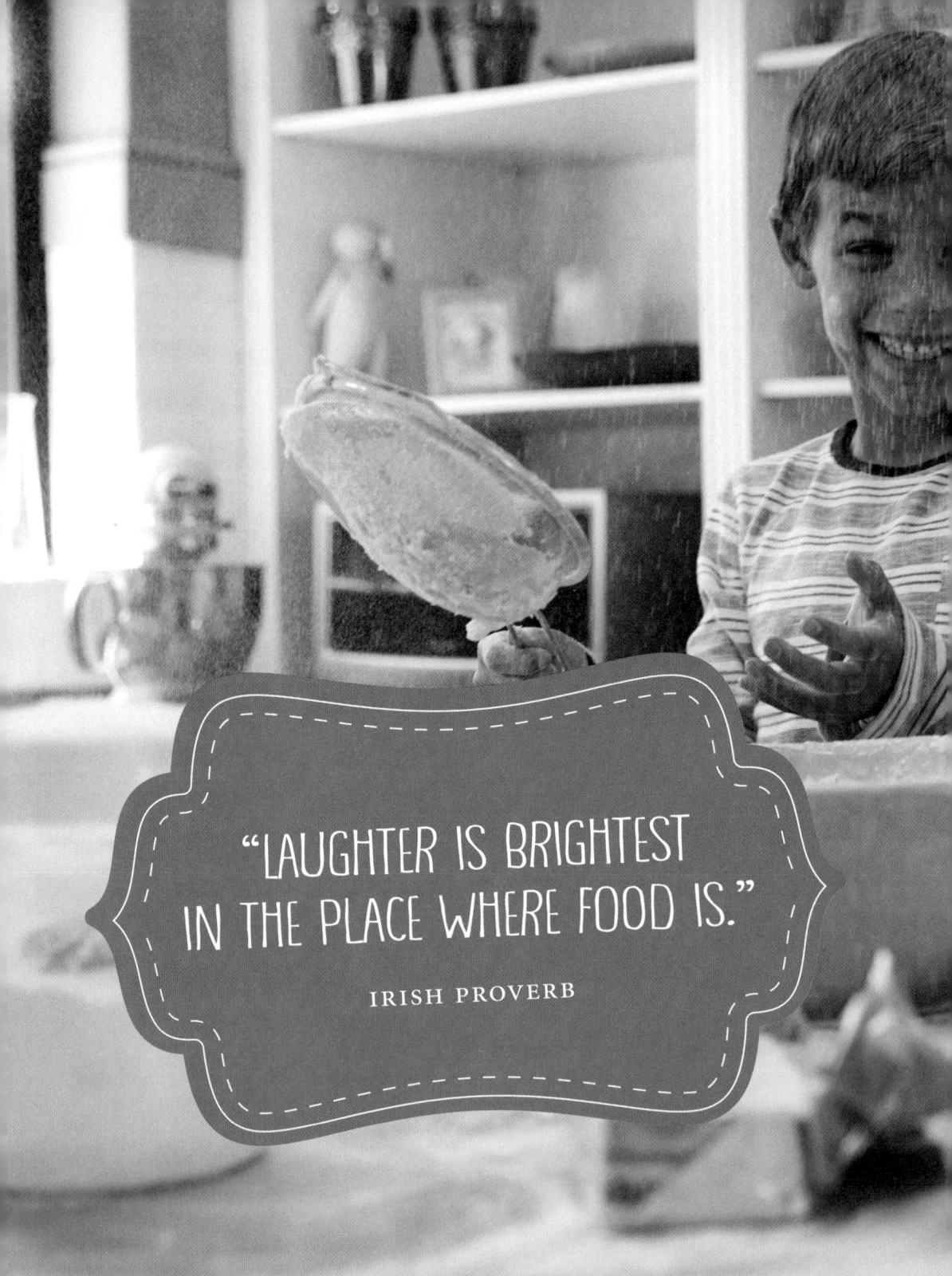

"If you want to be happy for a lifetime, plant a garden."

ANCIENT CHINESE PROVERB

"Good food
is the foundation
of genuine
happiness."

AUGUSTE ESCOFFIER,
The Escoffier Cookbook

"Meatballs are good news for cooks. Why? It's almost impossible to mess them up."

ELLEN BROWN, *The Complete Meatball Cookbook*

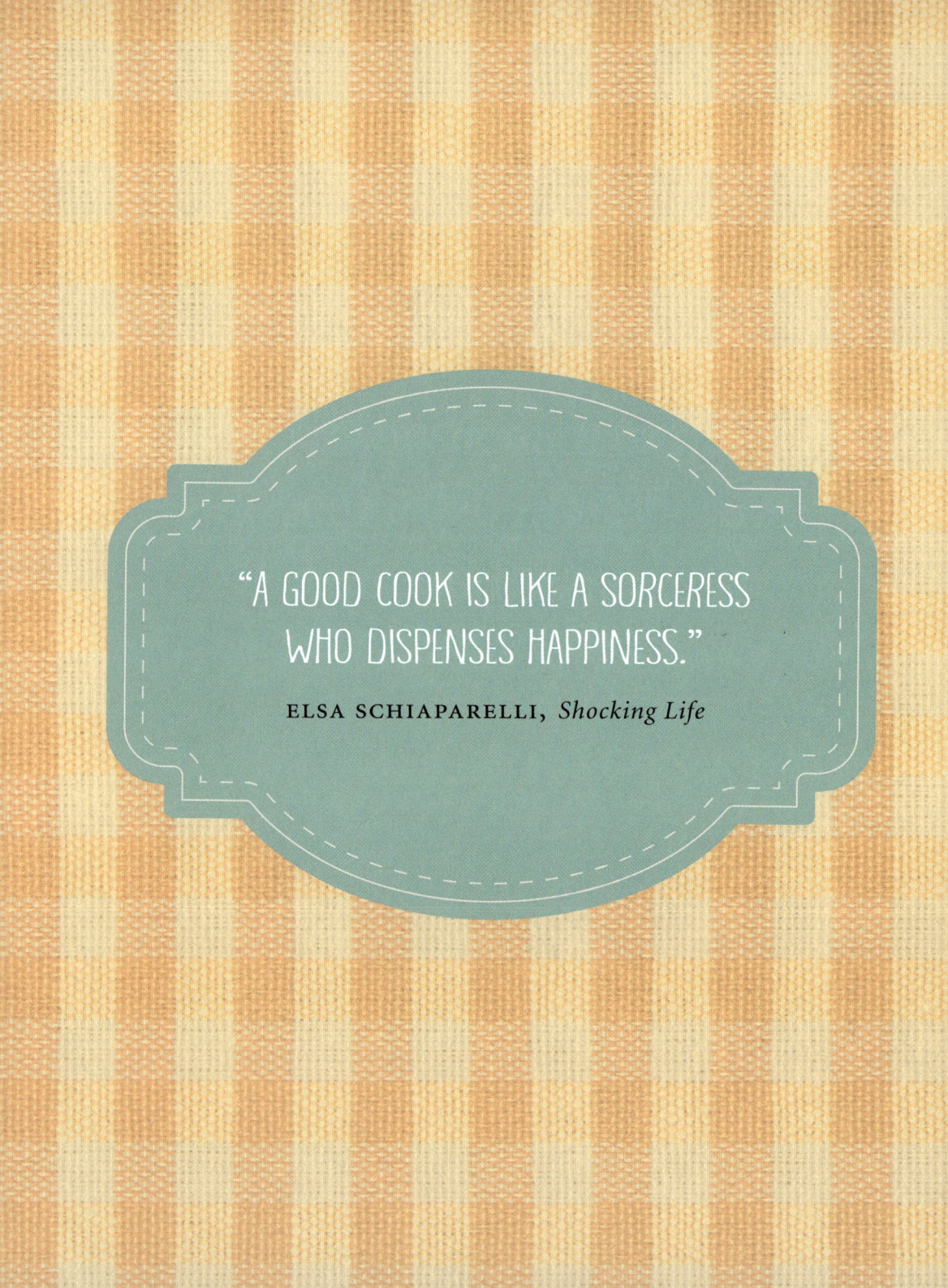

"A GOOD COOK IS LIKE A SORCERESS WHO DISPENSES HAPPINESS."

ELSA SCHIAPARELLI, *Shocking Life*

"The only time to eat diet food is while you're waiting for the steak to cook."

JULIA CHILD

"When you are making something in the kitchen, always make it with love. This is especially important when baking. If you bake a cake with negative thoughts it's almost guaranteed to fail. Always make food with love and you will taste the difference."

JOSÉ STICHBURY,
SWOON FOOD (WWW.SWOONFOOD.COM)

"All sorrows are less with bread."

MIGUEL DE CERVANTES, *Don Quixote*

"THE OTHER DAY A VALET TOLD ME HE'D ADDED BACON TO MY RECIPE FOR JALAPEÑO MUFFINS, AND I SAID, 'YES, THAT'S IT, DUDE! GO FOR IT!'"

GUY FIERI, *Food: Cookin' It, Livin' It, Lovin' It*

"A NICKEL WILL GET YOU ON THE SUBWAY,
BUT GARLIC WILL GET YOU A SEAT."

OLD NEW YORK PROVERB

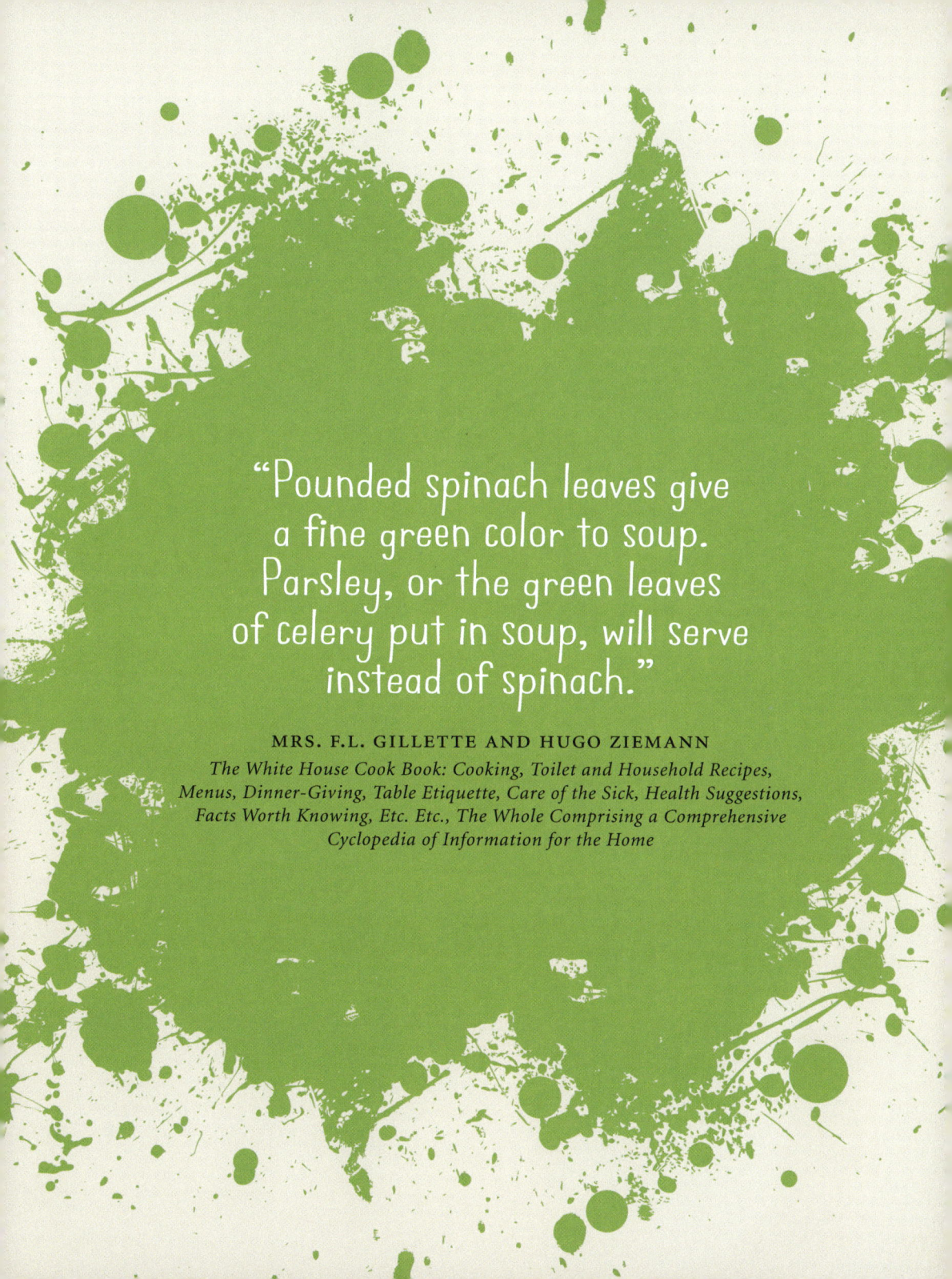

"Pounded spinach leaves give a fine green color to soup. Parsley, or the green leaves of celery put in soup, will serve instead of spinach."

MRS. F.L. GILLETTE AND HUGO ZIEMANN
The White House Cook Book: Cooking, Toilet and Household Recipes, Menus, Dinner-Giving, Table Etiquette, Care of the Sick, Health Suggestions, Facts Worth Knowing, Etc. Etc., The Whole Comprising a Comprehensive Cyclopedia of Information for the Home

"Dessert should be as delicious as it is beautiful. If you have to choose between the two, choose delicious, beautiful doesn't taste good on its own. And remember, you can never go wrong with whipped cream and sprinkles."

STACEY THIMMES, THE SUGAR COATED COTTAGE
(WWW.THESUGARCOATEDCOTTAGE.COM)

"In my kitchen nothing goes to waste! I freeze the rinds from Parmesan cheese and use them for flavoring dishes such as soups and sauces. The rind will not melt into the dishes, but it will impart flavor."

ELLEN BROWN, *The Sausage Cookbook Bible*

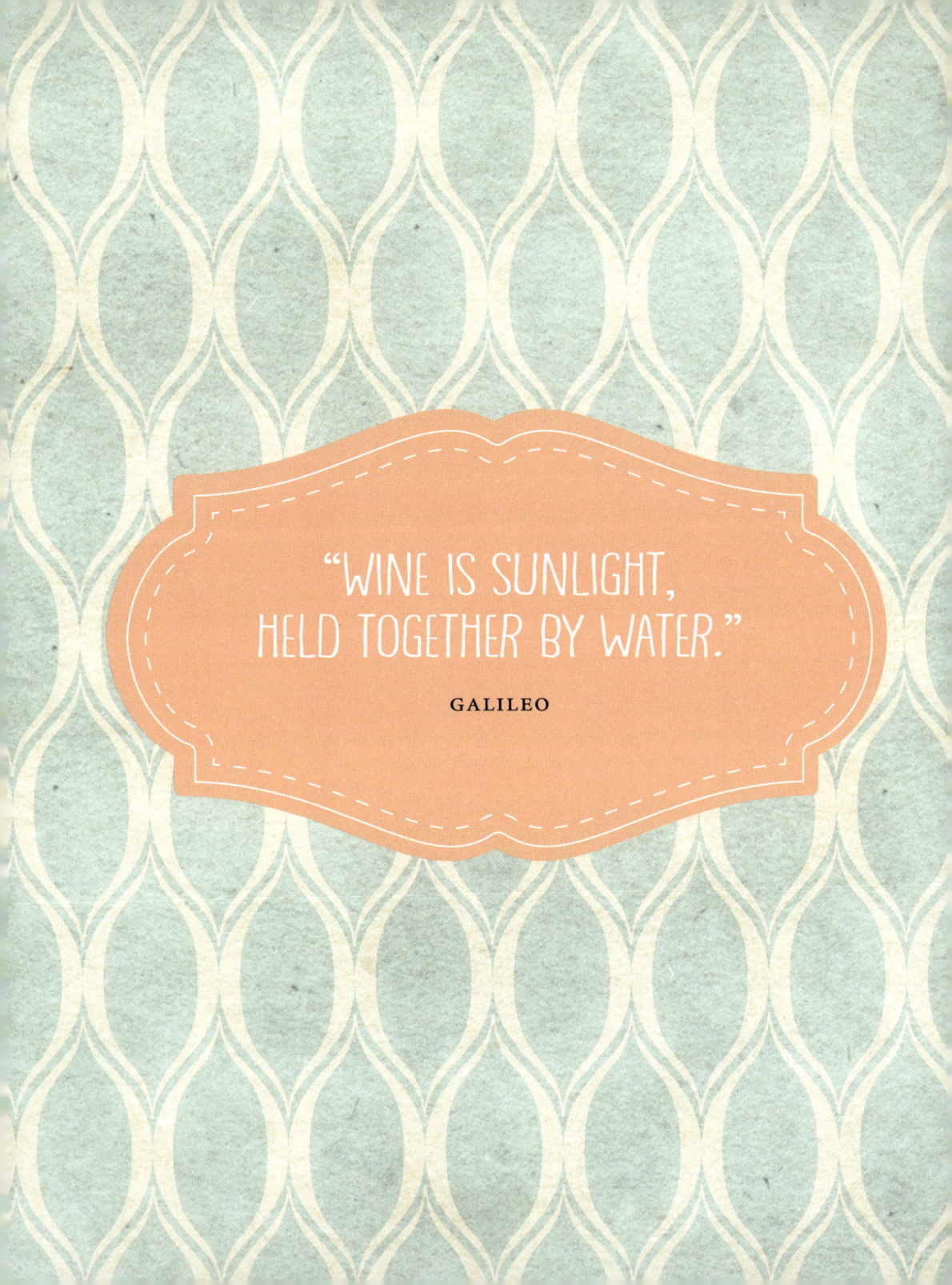

"A few choice flowers make a charming variety
in the appearance of even the most simply laid table,
and a pleasing variety at the table is quite as essential
to the enjoyment of the repast as is a good choice of dishes,
for the eye in fact should be gratified as much as the palate."

MRS. F.L. GILLETTE AND HUGO ZIEMANN
*The White House Cook Book: Cooking, Toilet and Household Recipes, Menus,
Dinner-Giving, Table Etiquette, Care of the Sick, Health Suggestions,
Facts Worth Knowing, Etc. Etc., The Whole Comprising a Comprehensive
Cyclopedia of Information for the Home*

"There are two activities in life
in which we can lovingly and carefully
put something inside of someone we love.
Cooking is the one we can do three times a day
for the rest of our lives, without pills.
In both activities, practice makes perfect."

MARIO BATALI, IN *Esquire* MAGAZINE

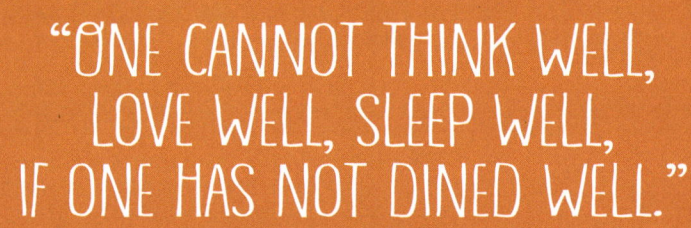

"One cannot think well, love well, sleep well, if one has not dined well."

VIRGINIA WOOLF,
A Room of One's Own

"A good cook is the peculiar gift of the gods.
He must be a perfect creature
from the brain to the palate,
from the palate to the finger's end."

WALTER SAVAGE LANDOR, *Imaginary Conversations*

"There is no such passion
in human nature,
as the passion for gravy
among commercial gentlemen."

CHARLES DICKENS,
The Life and Adventures of Martin Chuzzlewit

"For the best breakfast sandwich ever, cook the eggs in bacon fat."

TINA HAUPERT,
CARROTS 'N' CAKE

"There is no such thing as failure in the kitchen. Every time a recipe doesn't turn out as expected, you learn something new, which in turn, makes the next meal even better."

JESS HOLMES,
SWEETEST MENU (WWW.SWEETESTMENU.COM)

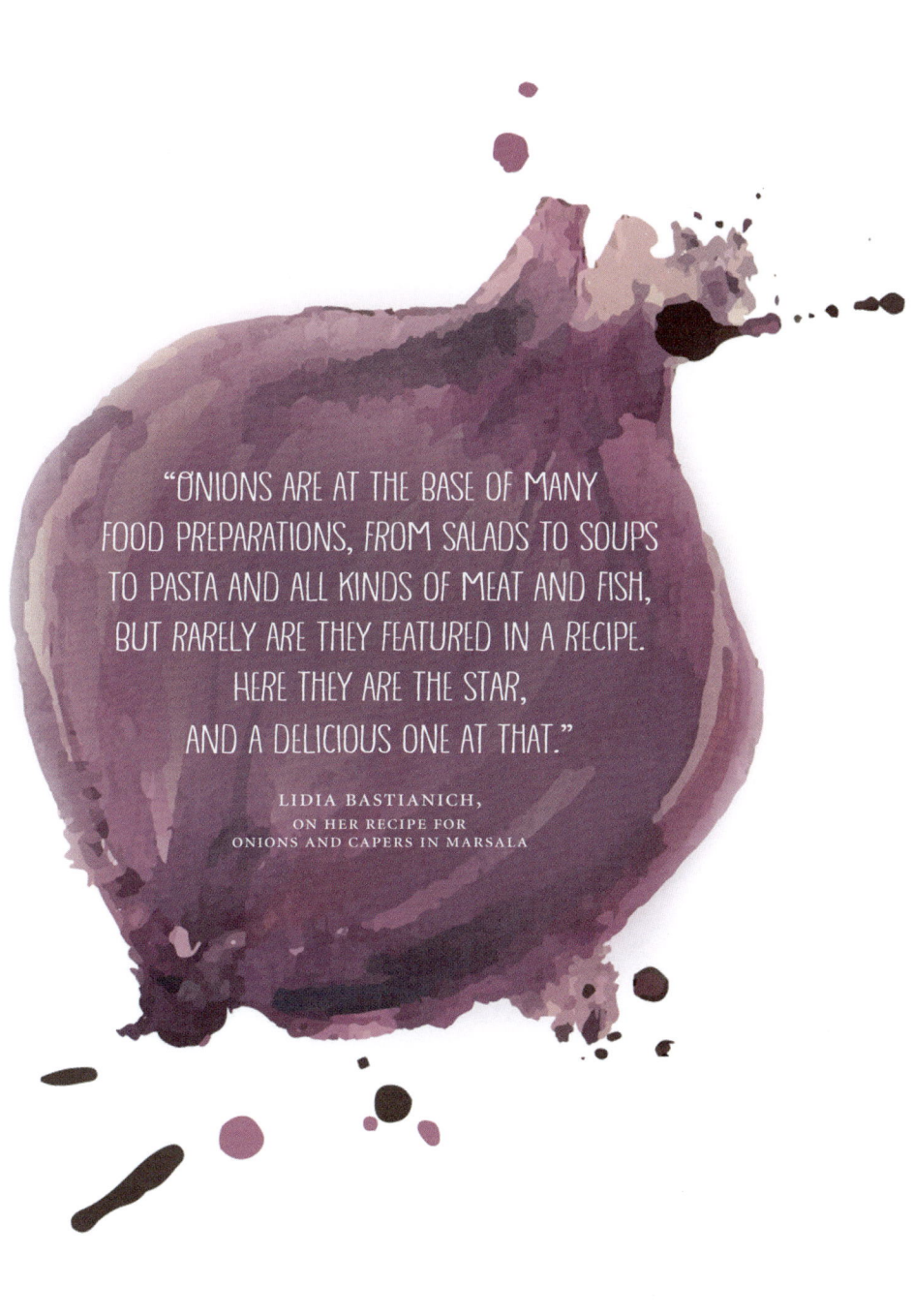

"ONIONS ARE AT THE BASE OF MANY FOOD PREPARATIONS, FROM SALADS TO SOUPS TO PASTA AND ALL KINDS OF MEAT AND FISH, BUT RARELY ARE THEY FEATURED IN A RECIPE. HERE THEY ARE THE STAR, AND A DELICIOUS ONE AT THAT."

LIDIA BASTIANICH,
ON HER RECIPE FOR
ONIONS AND CAPERS IN MARSALA

"There is not a thing that is more positive than bread."

FYODOR DOSTOYEVSKY

"This is my invariable advice to people: Learn how to cook—try new recipes, learn from your mistakes, be fearless, and above all have fun!"

JULIA CHILD, *My Life in France*

"The greatest delight the fields and woods minister is the suggestion of an occult relation between man and the vegetable. I am not alone and unacknowledged. They nod to me and I to them."

RALPH WALDO EMERSON

"Cauliflower is nothing but cabbage with a college education."

MARK TWAIN

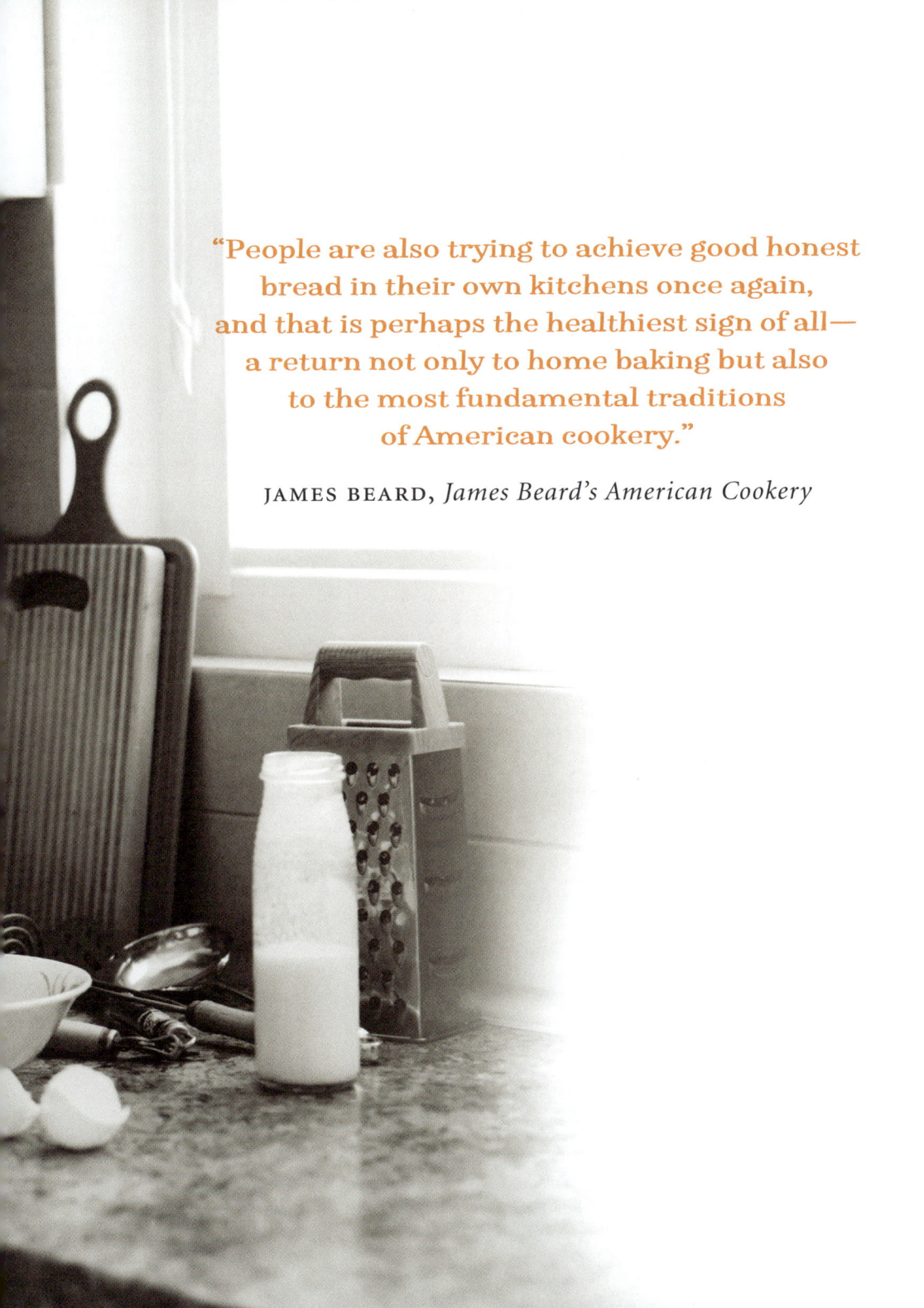

"People are also trying to achieve good honest bread in their own kitchens once again, and that is perhaps the healthiest sign of all— a return not only to home baking but also to the most fundamental traditions of American cookery."

JAMES BEARD, *James Beard's American Cookery*

"It's simple, I know, if it doesn't taste good, you won't eat it!"

MADHU GADIA,

AUTHOR OF *New Indian Home Cooking* AND *The Indian Vegan Kitchen* (WWW.CUISINEOFINDIA.COM)

"So long as you have food in your mouth,
you have solved all questions for the time being."

FRANZ KAFKA

"Lest you think you need a special occasion for a prime rib meal, rest assured, as far as your guests are concerned, prime rib is the occasion."

PETER KAMINSKY,
Prime: The Complete Prime Rib Cookbook

"When a cake sticks to a pan,
set it for a few minutes on a cloth
wrung out of cold water.
It will then come out in good shape."

The Kitchen Encyclopedia

"My mom always says, 'If you can read, you can cook.' It's true. Just pick up a recipe and give it a go!"

KATHRYN DOHERTY,
FAMILY FOOD ON THE TABLE
(WWW.FAMILYFOODONTHETABLE.COM)

"I hate people who are not serious about meals. It is so shallow of them."

OSCAR WILDE, *The Importance of Being Earnest*

"Nothing would be more tiresome than eating and drinking if God had not made them a pleasure as well as a necessity."

VOLTAIRE

"When my mother wanted to get to know someone new, or to maintain a friendship she cherished, she shared food. In my childhood home, food symbolized family, friendship, and love. It symbolizes them for me today."

TINKY WEISBLAT,
The Pudding Hollow Cookbook

"When it comes to healthy eating, food isn't black and white. It's gray. A glass of wine or a couple of Reese's Peanut Butter Cups can fit into a healthy diet the same way kale or salmon does."

TINA HAUPERT, CARROTS 'N' CAKE

"Puri-fried bread
makes any meal a celebration.
Everyone, young or old, enjoy puries.
Although you can make them alone,
they are easier to make with two people;
one fries and the other rolls."

MADHU GADIA,

AUTHOR OF *New Indian Home Cooking*
AND *The Indian Vegan Kitchen*
www.cusineofindia.com

"GOOD APPLE PIES ARE A CONSIDERABLE PART OF OUR DOMESTIC HAPPINESS."

JANE AUSTEN
IN A LETTER TO HER SISTER CASSANDRA
IN 1815

"A good cook is...an artist whom one may bless after having eaten the courses he has served, an officer who will make one's table the envy of all who have shared its good cheer, a seneschal of grave mien and imposing presence, conscientious in his work, prolific in resources, proud of his art, who gives dignity to his labours."

ISABELLA BEETON,
The Book of Household Management

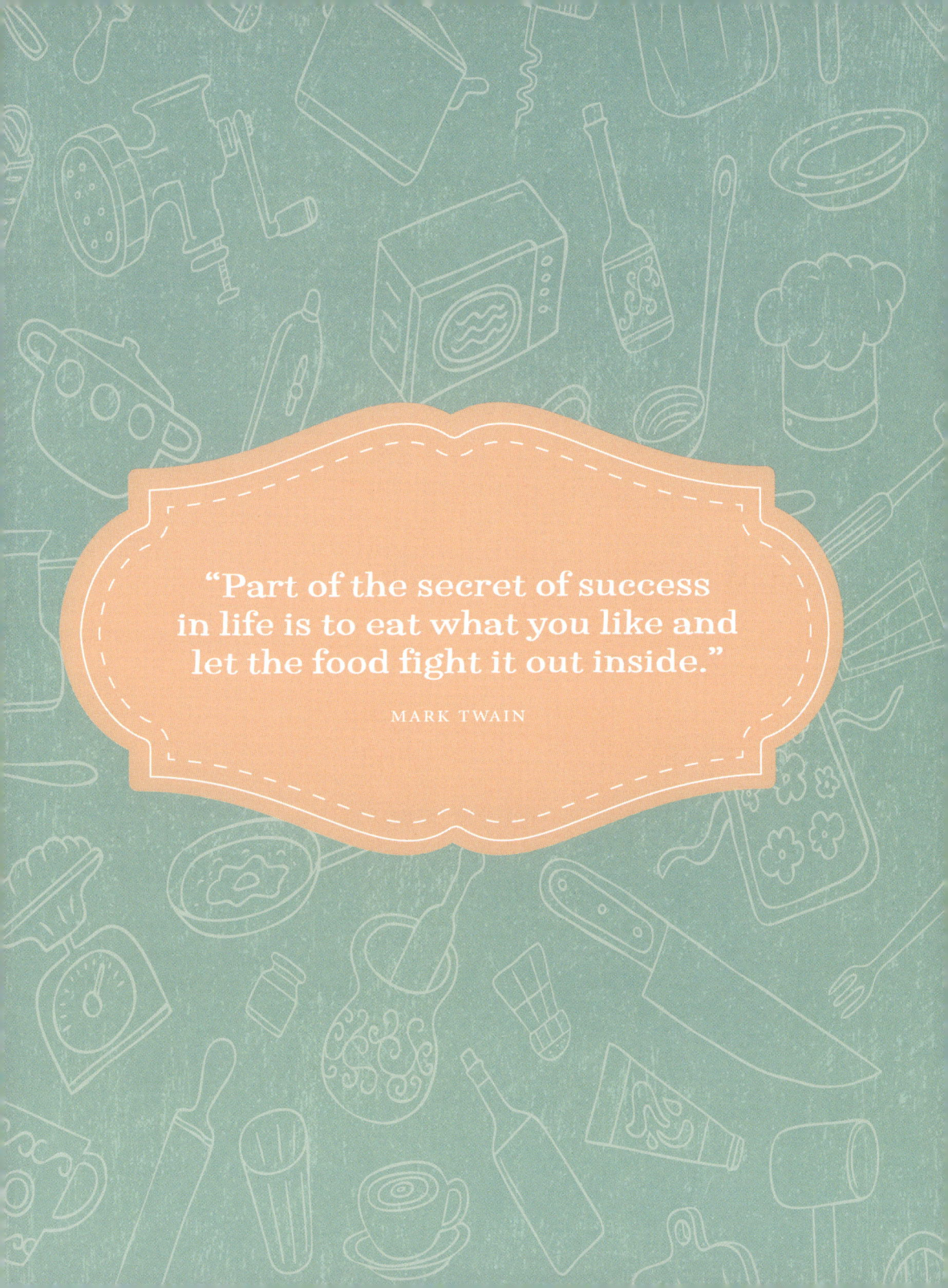

"Truly beautiful food is food that makes you look and feel amazing, inside and out."

JOSÉ STICHBURY,
SWOON FOOD (WWW.SWOONFOOD.COM)

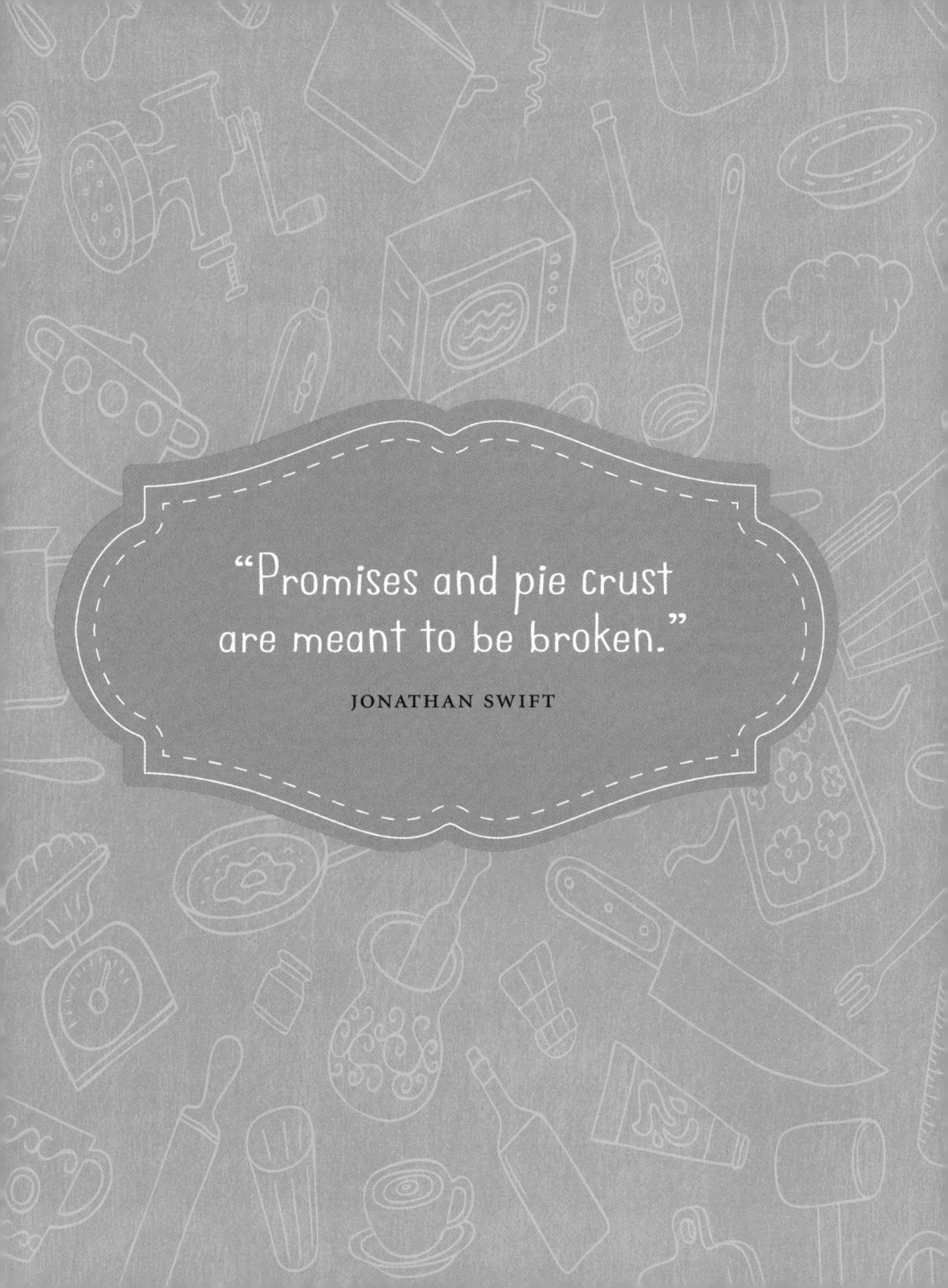

"Promises and pie crust are meant to be broken."

JONATHAN SWIFT

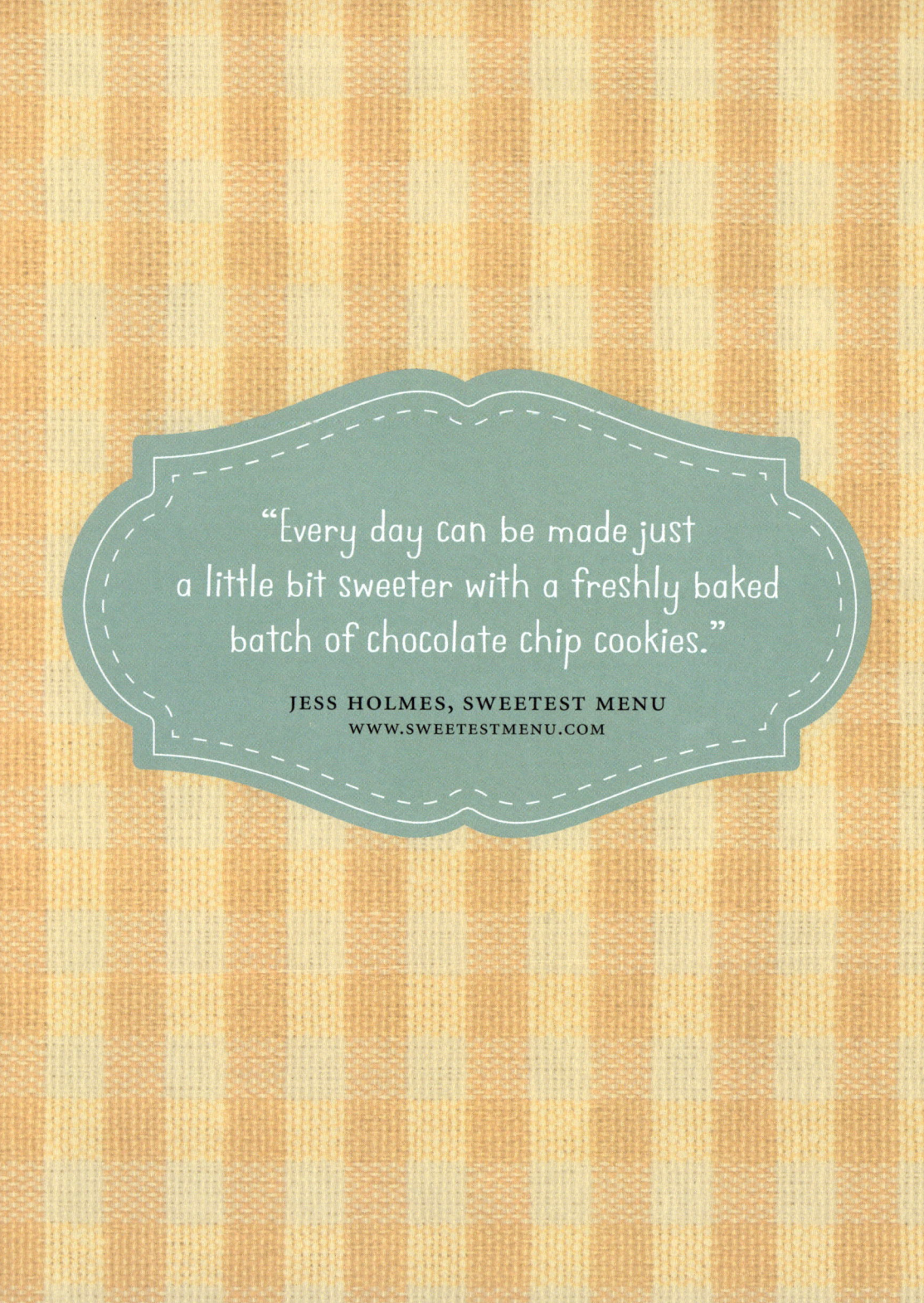

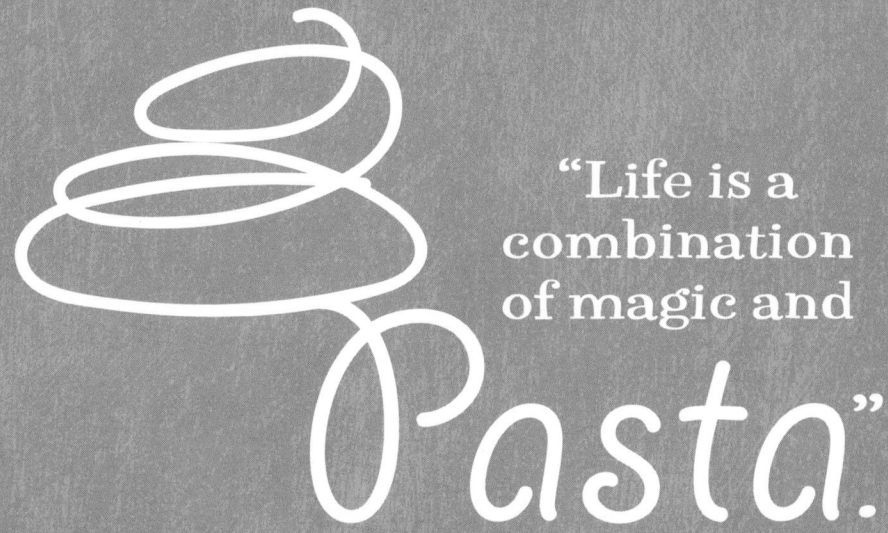

"Life is a combination of magic and Pasta."

FEDERICO FELLINI

"Fish should never be served without a salad of some kind."

RUFUS ESTES,
Good Things To Eat:
The First Cookbook by an African-American Chef

"Measure the girth of the chef and you can rate his restaurant."

FRENCH PROVERB

> "THE AMBITION OF EVERY GOOD COOK MUST BE TO MAKE SOMETHING VERY GOOD WITH THE FEWEST POSSIBLE INGREDIENTS."
>
> URBAIN DUBOIS

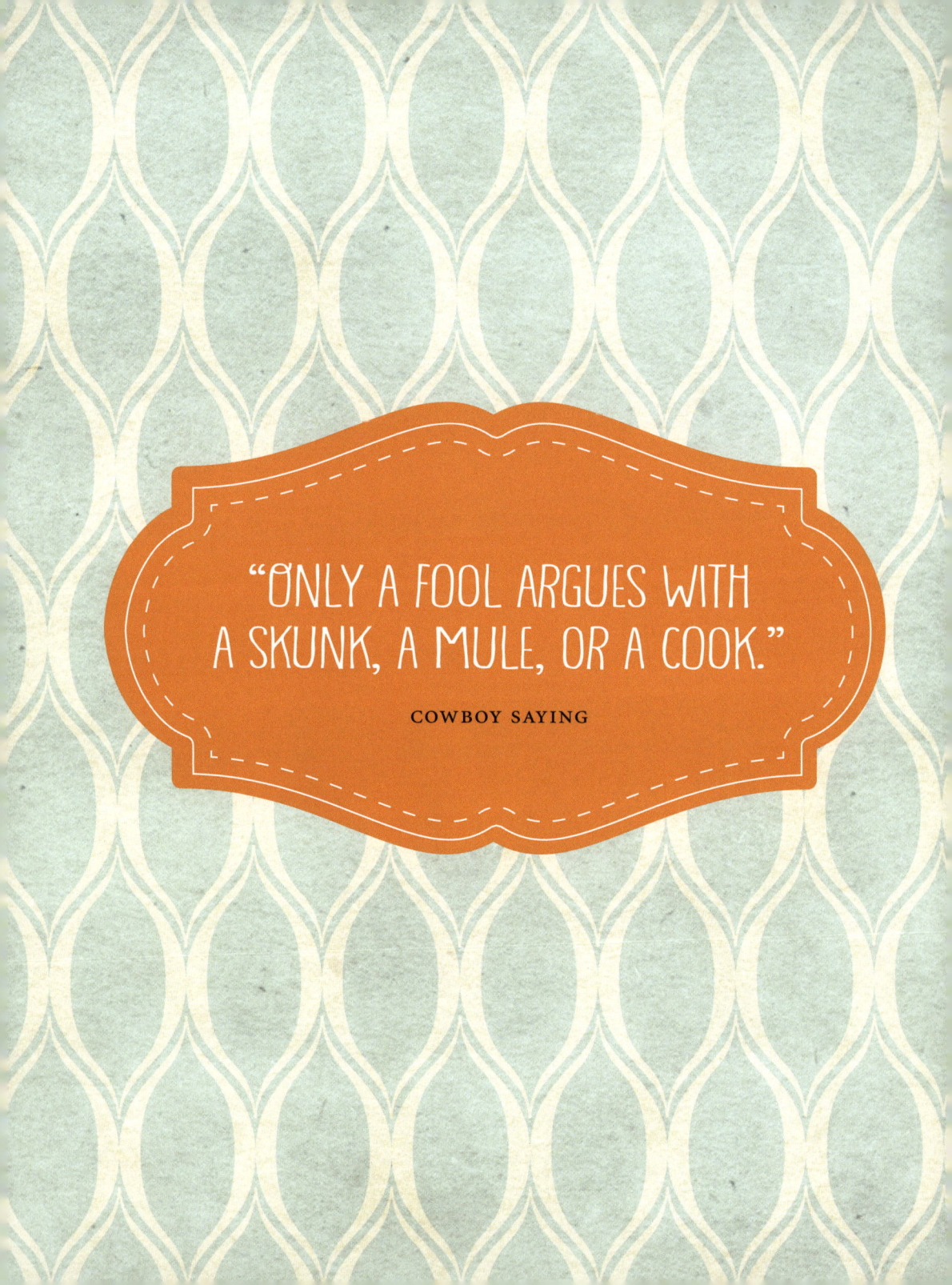

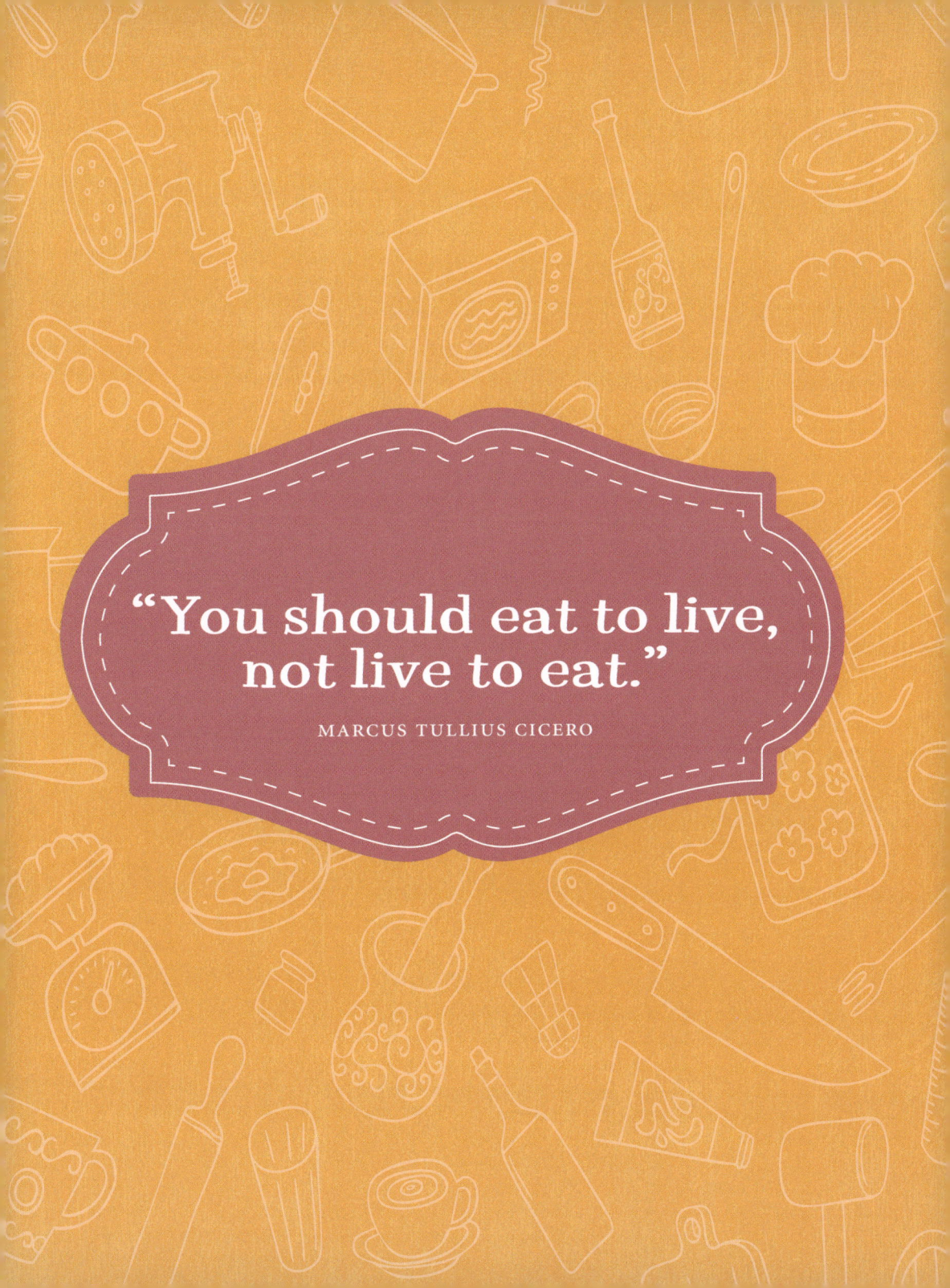

> "You should eat to live, not live to eat."
>
> MARCUS TULLIUS CICERO

"Nothing brightens the day like a glass of water with a big slice of lemon. Beautiful and delicious and so simple!"

"Candles on the table can make even leftovers feel special."

Any serious cook will tell you that having the right knives to work with is essential to your food preparation. The bottom line is, without a sharp knife of the right size and weight for the job, you will do twice the work to achieve your result—and your result will be unsatisfactory.

"The perfect crowd pleaser for a table of picky palates? Roast chicken!"

Roast Chicken

The smell of a chicken (or turkey) roasting in the oven is truly intoxicating, so that by the time the bird is cooked, you want to devour it instantly—crunchy skin first! Crunchy skin is important, and so is juicy, moist flesh. Here's a recipe with guaranteed results.

Makes 4 to 6 servings

Ingredients
1 4–6 pound chicken (see next page on using this recipe for turkey)
10–20 medium heads garlic, peeled
1 lemon
Salt and pepper
Poultry seasoning (a premade blend of thyme, sage, marjoram, rosemary, black pepper, and nutmeg)

Directions
- Preheat oven to 375°F.
- Remove the neck, giblets, and liver from the cavity of the chicken. See next page for possible uses.
- Rinse the chicken with cold water and pat it dry with paper towels. Place the chicken breast-side up in a roasting pan.
- Put the peeled garlic cloves in the cavity of the chicken. Cut the lemon in half, remove any seeds, and squirt the juice of one-half lemon over the chicken. Cut the squeezed lemon half into pieces and put them into the cavity with the garlic cloves.
- Sprinkle the chicken with salt and pepper and then lightly dust it with the poultry seasoning. Be sure to put the salt, pepper, and poultry seasoning into the cavity, too.
- Place the roasting dish in the oven and cook for 30 minutes. Lower the heat to 350°F and cook for another hour. Pull the pan out of the oven and test the bird for doneness. The legs should shake easily and when you pierce the lower part of the breast, near the thigh, the juices should run clear. If there is resistance in the leg and/or the juices are pink, put the chicken back in the oven. Check it every 10 to 15 minutes until the juices run clear. The skin will be brown and crispy. Resist the urge to take it out too soon!
- Remove the chicken to a warmed platter and let it sit for about 10 minutes before carving.

- Make a delicious gravy by putting the roasting pan over a burner on the oven, turning the burner to low, and using a fork to mix the juices with the cooked bits that are stuck to the pan. Sprinkle 1 Tablespoon of flour over the juices, using the fork to mash and blend the flour into the juices. Don't let the mixture come to a boil, just keep it warm, stirring the flour with the fork to break up any clumps. Add more flour if it's too runny, but avoid adding too much at once. When it's nice and smooth, season with salt and pepper, and pour into a gravy boat or small heat-proof pitcher.
- Carve the chicken and serve with the gravy.

To Do a Turkey

A turkey is just a large chicken and can be seasoned in the same way. The problem with a turkey is that by the time the innermost meat is cooked, the outer parts tend to be too dry. This method will prevent that, while also giving you crispy skin—essential!

Most turkeys weigh 12 to 14 pounds. Prep and season the bird as instructed for the chicken, put it in a large roasting pan, and stick some slivers of butter under the skin of the breast. Next, create a foil "tent" over the bird, which will keep it moist. Fashion the tent by cutting two large pieces of foil and folding them together along the longest side to create a crimped edge. Position the tent over the turkey and secure the edges around the roasting pan.

Roast at 375°F for 45 minutes before reducing the heat. Cook for another 90 minutes at 350°F, then remove the foil tent and continue to cook for another 30 minutes. Turn the heat up to 400°F for the last 15 minutes. Check for doneness in the same way as with the chicken: by "shaking" the legs and piercing the lower breast to see the color of the juice. If it needs more time, reduce the oven temperature to 350° and check it every 10 to 15 minutes.

Giblets, Liver, and Neck

Most people have no interest in these parts and just toss them. I like them all.
Here's what I do with them:

Take the neck out of the paper and rinse all parts under cold water. Place on a paper towel to absorb extra water. Cut the giblets and liver into nickel-sized pieces and put them around the chicken on the roasting pan. Put the neck into the cavity. When you reduce the oven temperature to 350°F, take the neck out of the cavity and put it in the pan with the other pieces. When the chicken is cooked, the juices have flowed into the pan, and you've removed the bird to a platter to make the gravy, remove the neck. As you're mashing the flour into the gravy, mash the cooked liver pieces, too, so they combine with the gravy. The gravy will be so much tastier with the addition of the giblets and liver!

Roasting Origins

The process of roasting in an oven evolved
from cooking meat on a spit over a fire.
The fire needed to be tended to maintain the heat,
and the spit needed to be turned during
the entire cooking time. Turning the spit was done
by the lowest person on the kitchen-help totem pole,
and even in some places, by trained dogs!

Onions are a vital element of the
perfect meatloaf recipe. Your eyes may tear
when you chop or dice raw onion,
as the vegetable secretes a substance
called lachrymator when cut.
This combines with the moisture in the eye
to produce a weak sulfuric acid solution.
To avoid this, use a really sharp knife,
which minimizes the secretion.
If it's still a problem, wear light goggles.

Can't Miss Meatloaf

A good meatloaf is a piece of heaven—moist, flavorful, succulent, and savory. It's delicious just out of the oven, and the leftovers make great sandwiches. A tried-and-true recipe is one that includes Quaker® Oats. And ketchup, of course. Here it is.

Makes 1 loaf

Ingredients
1 ½ pounds lean ground beef
¾ cup Quaker® Oats (quick or old-fashioned, uncooked)
¾ cup finely chopped onion (the finer the better)
½ cup ketchup
1 egg, lightly beaten
1 Tablespoon Worcestershire sauce
2 cloves garlic, minced
½ teaspoon salt
¼ teaspoon black pepper

Directions
- Preheat oven to 350°F.
- In a large bowl, mix all ingredients lightly but thoroughly. Shape meat mixture into a loaf and place on a cookie sheet.
- Bake 50 to 55 minutes.

A Medley of Mix-Ins
If you want to jazz up your meatloaf, consider adding any of the following:
- Substitute salsa for the ketchup and add 2 Tablespoons chopped fresh cilantro
- Swap your favorite hot sauce for the Worcestershire sauce
- Shred 2 carrots in a food processor, squeeze dry, and add to the meat mixture
- Substitute spicy V8 juice for the ketchup
- Add 1 jalapeño pepper, finely chopped
- Add ½ green or red pepper, minced

"Every family needs simple, foolproof recipes for those frenzied weeknights. Enchiladas are a great go-to, an easy dinner to throw together for the family after a busy day."

Chicken Enchiladas

In Mexico, an enchilada is simply a corn tortilla with filling that's baked and covered with a pepper sauce. Keep cans of black beans, green chilies, refried beans, black olives, and other Mexican food essentials on hand so you know you can make these with the simple addition of leftover chicken—or ground beef, pulled pork, sausage, or even rice or potatoes for vegetarian options.

Makes 4 servings of 2 each

2 Tablespoons vegetable oil
1 onion, diced
1–2 pounds boneless, skinless chicken breasts, diced into ½-inch pieces (or use precooked shredded chicken)
Salt and pepper to taste
1 4-ounce can diced green chilies
1 15.5-ounce can black beans
8 large flour or corn tortillas
3 cups shredded cheese, preferably cheddar and pepper jack
2 10-ounce cans enchilada sauce
2 Tablespoons cilantro, chopped (optional)
1 jalapeño, diced (optional)
1 Tablespoon chipotle (optional)
1 Tablespoon hot sauce of your liking (optional)

Directions

- Preheat oven to 350°F.
- Add the oil to a large skillet over medium-high heat. Add the onion and sauté until translucent, about 3 minutes. If using uncooked chicken, add it and the green chilies to the skillet. Stir together and sauté, stirring occasionally, until chicken pieces are cooked through, about 8 minutes. If using pre-cooked chicken, just add the chilies when the onions are translucent, and sauté together for about 5 minutes, then add the pre-cooked chicken and stir to heat through, another 2 minutes. Remove from heat and set aside. Season with salt and pepper.
- Put the beans and cheese in separate bowls with spoons so you can assemble the enchiladas.

- Put the beans and cheese in separate bowls with spoons so you can assemble the enchiladas.
- Doing one tortilla at a time, open one can of enchilada sauce and spread about 2 Tablespoons enchilada sauce over the surface of the tortilla. Spoon beans down the middle, then spoon some of the chicken-chili mixture over the beans, and top with cheese. Roll up the tortilla and put it in a greased 9x12 baking dish. Fill and roll the remaining tortillas. Open the second can of enchilada sauce and drizzle it over the enchiladas in the baking dish. Top with additional cheese.
- Bake uncovered for about 20 minutes. Be careful not to overcook them.
- Garnish with chopped cilantro and serve.

Pump It Up!

For more fiery flavor, add the chopped jalapeño in with the chicken-onion-chili mixture in the last couple minutes of sautéeing. You can also doctor your enchilada sauce to make everything hotter and more flavorful. Add a Tablespoon (or more!) of your favorite hot sauce or the chipotle—or both. Experiment with different kinds of peppers and cheeses, using increasingly hotter peppers, like habaneros, or more of a hot cheese and less cheddar. Of course, be mindful of the company you're serving the enchiladas. If your family doesn't share your passion for heat, make them as instructed, and put hot sauces on the table.

Sauté Wordplay

The word sauté comes from the French "to jump." In the kitchen, it refers to cooking foods in a skillet over high heat. You know your pan is hot enough when the liquid or fat added to it to begin the cooking process actually "jumps" in the pan.

The best oils to use for frying are
canola, corn, and peanut. They can sustain
the highest heats without darkening or burning.
You can fry in a cast-iron skillet or other heavy-bottomed,
deep-sided skillet if you're frying something relatively
flat or shallow, like chicken pieces or thin pieces of meat.
Use a deep-frying thermometer to gauge the temperature
of the oil, as it needs to be constant.

Fabulous Fried Chicken

If you have trouble getting your family together to the table for dinner, make fried chicken. They will come running! It's time-consuming and it's messy, and there is a lot of cleanup. You'll also need to invest in a thermometer that can be put into the hot oil and a meat thermometer, if you don't have them already. But is all that worth it? Most definitely, yes! The secret is to let the chicken marinate in the buttermilk for several hours, preferably overnight. The easiest way to do this so you don't have to think too much about it is on the day before you want to make the fried chicken, immediately prep the chicken pieces after you've finished dinner. Then you can go to bed and not worry about it until the next day.

Makes 6 to 8 servings

Ingredients
2 cups buttermilk
2 Tablespoons Frank's Red Hot sauce (or hot sauce of your preference)
1 Tablespoon salt
2–3 pounds chicken pieces, with skin
2 cups all-purpose flour
1 ½ teaspoons baking powder
1 teaspoon ground black pepper
1 teaspoon paprika
5 cups peanut oil (preferable), vegetable oil, or canola oil (not olive oil)

Directions
The night before:
- In a large bowl, combine buttermilk, hot sauce, and 1 teaspoon of the salt. Pour the liquid into a 2- to 2 ½-gallon self-sealing plastic bag. Add the chicken pieces, dunking them so they all get coated with the liquid. Seal the bag, pressing out any excess air. Put the bag in a bowl or on a plate and put it in the refrigerator.

The day of:

- Before leaving the house in the morning, turn the bag with the chicken pieces over so the liquid gets to all the pieces.
- Take the chicken out of the refrigerator 30 minutes before you plan to get started with the coating and frying.
- To make the coating, combine the flour, baking powder, black pepper, paprika, and 2 teaspoons of salt in a large pie plate. Line a 9x12 baking dish with waxed paper.
- Remove the chicken pieces from the buttermilk, shaking off excess liquid. Dredge each piece in the flour mixture. Place the pieces on the lined baking pan. Put a second piece of waxed paper on the dredged pieces. Discard excess buttermilk mixture.
- Using a large cast-iron skillet, an electric skillet, a heavy stainless-steel skillet, or a Dutch oven, pour about ½-inch of oil in the skillet. Heat over medium until the oil reaches 360°F.
- Using tongs, place 4 or 5 pieces in to fry, skin side down. Don't crowd the pieces. Cook about 5 minutes, until the pieces are golden brown on the bottom. Carefully turn them using the tongs. Continue to cook for 5 minutes, then flip again and cook another 4 to 5 minutes, depending on the size of the piece. The internal temperature of the chicken should be 160°F at the meatiest part, and the juices should run clear when pierced with a knife. Transfer cooked pieces to a cookie sheet lined with paper towels and cover with a clean dishtowel to keep warm.
- Cook in batches, maintaining the temperature and level of the oil as you go, and removing any floating bits of skin and coating. Be careful not to let the oil get too hot.

"My favorite thing about frying is that you can fry almost anything! Pickles, butter, basil—even Oreos! You name it, you can probably fry it!"

"Everyone should experience making bread in their life. It is elemental, essential, and exhilarating."

The Best BBQ Ribs

Ribs require three things to be really great: a flavorful rub, slow cooking time so the meat is tender, and finishing on a grill. You'll need to allow several hours for baking, and then about an hour between baking and grilling (as the ribs need to chill first), so factor that into your meal preparation schedule. Barbecue sauce is used during the grilling and there are so many on the market now that I like to use two different kinds so there's more variety and my family or guests can decide which they like better. Here's an easy recipe to get you started.

Makes 4 servings

Ingredients
4 pounds baby back pork ribs
1 Tablespoon salt
2 teaspoons dry mustard
2 teaspoons garlic powder
2 teaspoons paprika (mild or hot, your preference)
¼ teaspoon cayenne pepper
¼ teaspoon ground black pepper
1–2 cups store-bought barbecue sauce

Directions
- Preheat oven to 350°F.
- Using either heavy-duty aluminum foil or a double layer of foil, place each rack of ribs on foil.
- If there's a membrane on the ribs, slice into it with a sharp knife and pull it off.
- In a small bowl, combine the salt, dry mustard, paprika, cayenne pepper, and black pepper. Using your hands, sprinkle and rub the spice combination evenly over both sides of the ribs.
- Cover the ribs with another piece (or pieces) of foil, and place them on cookie sheets.
- Pop the sheets into the oven and bake for 2 hours without disturbing them. After you take them out of the oven, let sit for a couple of minutes. Unwrap and transfer to a cutting board or baking dish large enough to hold them. Pour the juices from the ribs into a heat-proof bowl or large measuring cup and set aside.

- Let the ribs cool completely, then rewrap them in foil and put them in the refrigerator. They will hold together on the grill better if they are chilled. Allow them to chill for 45–60 minutes.
- Light the grill and set it on high.
- Stir the barbeque sauce into the juices from the ribs. Grill the ribs, basting with the sauce and turning often so that they get covered and charred in places without burning. Grill for about 10 minutes.
- To serve, cut between the ribs, slather with some more sauce if desired, or put the remaining sauce on the table.

"The secret ingredient to truly great barbecue? Patience."

What Should I Braise?

Where roasting is cooking with dry heat,
braising is cooking with moist heat.
It differs from poaching and boiling in that the meat
is browned before undergoing the full cooking process.
Braising is a great way to flavor and tenderize
tough or gamey cuts of meat, be they beef, chicken,
pork, lamb, venison, duck, pheasant, buffalo, bear,
and so on. Certain vegetables are delicious braised
rather than steamed, including green beans, carrots,
beets, sweet potatoes, kale, collards, and cabbage.
Stews are fabulous concoctions of braised foods.

"When in doubt,
consider the slow cooker:
add your ingredients,
some broth or sauce, set on Low,
and come back in 6 to 8 hours.
You almost can't go wrong."

Herbed Pork Roast

This is a great meal to make in the fall. Serve with homemade applesauce and buttered noodles. Pork is a best friend of garlic, and this recipe calls for plenty of it! Between that and the fresh herbs, by the time this dish is cooked, everyone's mouths will be watering from the aroma.

Makes 6 to 8 servings

Ingredients
1 2-pound boneless pork roast
6 cloves garlic, minced
¼ cup fresh rosemary, chopped
2 Tablespoons fresh parsley, chopped
2 Tablespoons fresh sage, chopped
Salt and pepper to taste
3 ribs celery, cut into 4-inch lengths
⅓ cup chicken stock or broth

Directions
- Rinse pork and pat dry with paper towels. Combine garlic, rosemary, parsley, sage, salt, and pepper in a mixing bowl. Cut deep slits into the pork and stuff half of mixture into the slits. Rub remaining mixture on the outside of the roast.
- Arrange celery slices in the bottom of the slow cooker to form a bed for the meat.
- Preheat the oven broiler and line a broiler pan with heavy-duty aluminum foil. Broil pork for 3 minutes per side, until well browned. Transfer pork to the slow cooker and pour in any juices that have collected in the pan. Pour stock over pork.
- Cover and cook on High for about 2 hours, then reduce heat to Low and cook for 4 hours, until pork is fork tender. Carve pork into slices and moisten with juices from the slow cooker.

Broiling First is Best
Browning meat under the broiler accomplishes two things when using a slow cooker: It gives the meat a more appealing color and it heats it so that it passes through the "danger zone" of 40°F to 140°F faster, especially if you're cooking on Low.

"Almost all fish taste better with the skin on and the bones in."

Fabulous Fish

For anyone who's intimidated about how to cook fresh fish, this recipe is the answer. Because the fish cooks in a foil pouch, there is none of the smell or mess of frying. And the fish comes out moist and delicious.

Makes 4 to 6 servings

Ingredients
1.5 pounds salmon filet (or 1–2 pounds of your fish of choice)
1 lemon, cut in half, seeds removed
1 Tablespoon butter
Salt and pepper
¼ cup dry white wine

Directions
- Preheat the oven to 375°F.
- Line a cookie sheet with foil, cutting it long enough to extend over the sides. Cut another piece slightly larger, to be placed over the fish when it's prepared.
- Place the fish filet on the foil (if the filet has skin, put it skin side down).
- Squeeze half the lemon over the fish, then sprinkle with salt and pepper. Cut the butter into three slivers and place them on top of the filet, about an inch or so apart. Pour the wine over the fish.
- Put the other piece of foil over the fish. Line up the edges of the foil and fold and crimp them together so you form a pouch for the fish.
- Bake for 30 to 45 minutes depending on the thickness of the filet(s). Thinner fish needs less time.
- Remove the cookie sheet from the oven and let sit for a couple of minutes. Open around the seams. Place on a warm serving dish with slices of lemon and drizzle the juices over the fish.

Citrus flavors pair perfectly with fish.
Top off a fish dish with some lemon
or orange zest to make it a winner.
Zest (the finely shredded outer skin)
provides loads of flavor without being intrusive.

Crab Cakes

These are so tasty and fun to make and eat that the recipe had to be included in this book. The patties can be made ahead of time and refrigerated for up to one day until ready to cook. Wear an apron when it's time to cook them—they need to be fried in a skillet.

Makes 8 burger-sized patties

Ingredients
½ cup mayonnaise
1 large egg, beaten
1 Tablespoon Dijon mustard
1 Tablespoon Worcestershire sauce
½ teaspoon cayenne pepper
1 Tablespoon finely minced parsley
1 cup crushed saltine crackers
1 pound jumbo lump crabmeat, picked over
¼–½ cup vegetable oil

Directions
- In a small bowl, stir together the mayonnaise, egg, mustard, Worcestershire sauce, cayenne pepper, and parsley. In a large bowl, lightly mix the crab meat with the crushed crackers. Add the mayonnaise mixture and gently stir to combine. Refrigerate for at least one hour.
- Make the patties by dividing the mixture into eight portions and shaping into discs. Place them on a plate lined with parchment or waxed paper, and separate layers with same.
- In a large skillet (preferably cast iron), heat about ¼ cup of the oil until hot but not smoking. Place as many patties as will fit without crowding (3 or 4). Cook over medium-high heat for 3–4 minutes per side, until golden brown on both sides and heated through. Transfer cooked patties to a platter and cover with foil to keep warm while cooking the remaining patties. Add additional oil if needed to cook through the batches.
- Serve immediately with fresh lemon, cocktail sauce, or tartar sauce. Or sprinkle with Old Bay seasoning if desired.

Sauces and Other Deliciousness
If you're inspired, you can make your own cocktail sauce with ketchup, horseradish, and lemon juice, but I find that a high-quality jarred sauce is perfectly fine (and can be doctored with additional horseradish or hot sauce). Same goes for tartar sauce, which is essentially mayonnaise, relish, and salt and pepper. This is a great recipe to make for a cocktail party, as you can form the mixture into smaller cakes and serve as finger food with dipping sauces. Reduce cooking time on smaller patties.

"A well-put-together meal is an art form."

We think of curry as an Indian or Southeast Asian
dish featuring a spicy sauce. While this is mostly true,
curry is actually a combination of spices,
and in Indian cuisine the exact proportions are
often family secrets, with chefs priding themselves
on proprietary blends.

Curry Toppings
Traditionally, curries are served with a variety of toppings for people to choose from. Some that pair particularly well with a shrimp curry are flaked coconut, chutney, raisins, chopped salted peanuts, and fresh pineapple pieces.

Amazing Shrimp Curry

To make a delicious curry, all you need to do is purchase fresh curry powder in the spice section of your local market. It's a blend of cumin, turmeric, fenugreek, coriander, and chili peppers, and is a lovely golden color. This recipe makes a simple but delicious curry that the whole family can enjoy. Guaranteed!

Serves 4

Ingredients
1 cup chicken broth
1 cup milk
3 Tablespoons butter
½ onion, minced
2 teaspoons curry powder
3 Tablespoons flour
½ teaspoon kosher salt
½ teaspoon sugar
½ teaspoon ground ginger
2 cups cooked shrimp, cut into ¼-inch pieces
4 cups cooked white, brown, or jasmine rice

Directions
- Put the chicken broth and milk in a small saucepan and heat over low until just warmed.
- In a high-sided skillet, melt the butter over medium heat and add the onion and curry powder. Stir to cook the onion and coat it with the curry, about 2 to 3 minutes. Stir in the flour, salt, sugar, and ground ginger until onion bits are covered and flour is lumpy. Reduce the heat to low. Start adding the warmed chicken broth-milk mixture, stirring constantly after each addition to completely blend the liquid with the solids before adding more. Continue adding the liquid and stirring to combine. When all the liquid is added and the sauce is smooth, increase the heat to medium-high and continue cooking and stirring until sauce thickens, about 3 minutes.
- Stir in the cooked shrimp. Transfer the curry to a bowl to serve over the rice.

"If you want to reawaken your palette, eat a meal blindfolded. Search for and savor every bite."

"There's something magical about flipping pancakes and seeing the lightly browned surface, smelling the cakey, buttery smell, and watching the batter rise up ever so slightly as the other side cooks."

"Just because you can buy it in a bottle doesn't mean you shouldn't make it from scratch! Homemade salad dressings are easy, fresh, and delicious—everyone should have a go-to dressing recipe in their back pocket!"

Vinaigrette Salad Dressing

It's all about the proportion of oil to vinegar for a delightful salad dressing. The other trick is to make the dressing just before serving the salad. Don't refrigerate it or even let it sit out on the counter for too long. The fresher the better. And be sure to use kosher salt and freshly ground black pepper.

Makes approximately ½ cup, or enough to dress a leafy salad for 4

Ingredients
¼ cup fruity, extra-virgin olive oil
2 Tablespoons red wine vinegar
1 teaspoon kosher salt
½ teaspoon freshly ground black pepper

Directions
- In a bowl large enough to allow for vigorous stirring, combine the olive oil, vinegar, salt, and pepper. Using a fork, whisk the ingredients together until thoroughly combined.
- Pour the dressing over the salad ingredients and toss lightly. Serve.

Vinaigrette Variations
Dijon mustard: Add ½ teaspoon and stir in with other ingredients. This is nice when the salad contains some bitter greens, or if you like a little extra oomph to your dressing.
Garlic: Crush 1 peeled clove into the dressing. Garlic is tasty and good for you. Always a welcome addition for my family.
Herbs: Add ½ teaspoon dried herbs to the dressing, such as Italian seasoning or Herbes de Provence. Fresh herbs in the salad mix are nice, too—in moderation. Consider a Tablespoon of chopped fresh parsley, tarragon, or dill if the salad has cucumbers.
Pepper: Experiment with different kinds of peppercorns or even a combination of them to see if something tickles your tastebuds more than just black peppercorns. Other common peppercorns are green, white, and pink. Green peppercorns are harvested when young. They have a milder flavor than black peppercorns, which are harvested about midway to maturity. White peppercorns are harvested when most mature, and then soaked to remove their outer casing. White peppercorns have the most intense flavor of these three. Pink peppercorns are not technically peppercorns—they are the berries of a tree. They are softer than peppercorns and their flavor is more pungent but not necessarily more fiery. All the peppercorns can be purchased separately or in combinations.

A Perfect Salad?
Salad these days can be anything from simple greens to a hodgepodge of nearly anything and everything in the produce section of your local market. The most refreshing salad is one of a selection of super fresh, delicate greens. Boston Bibb lettuce is great with some crunchy romaine, baby spinach, and baby arugula. Use 6 to 8 cups of leaves for a salad for 4 people.

Why Poach an Egg?

An egg cooked by this method is free of the fat used to fry or even scramble it. The poaching should yield a soft, hot center and a firm white. Poached eggs are classically served atop toast or an English muffin rather than beside it so that every drop of yolk is absorbed by the bread. Poaching is achieved by breaking the egg into hot water. You can't just do that, though. The water needs vinegar in it so the egg whites will coagulate and set.

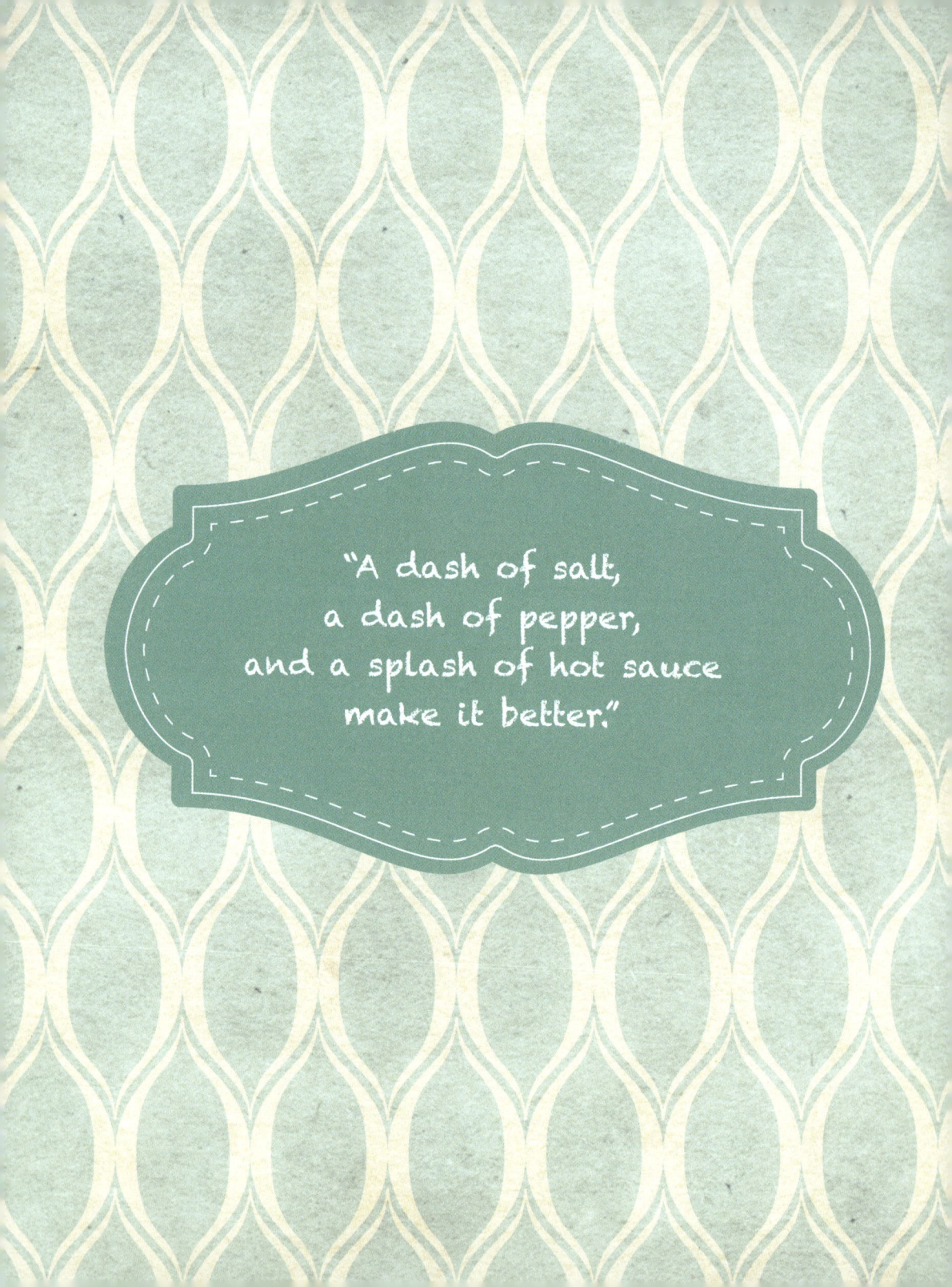

"A dash of salt, a dash of pepper, and a splash of hot sauce make it better."

"If there's elbow room at your Thanksgiving table,
you forgot to invite someone."

Macaroni and Cheese

One of the all-time best comfort foods, you can serve this creamy, delicious dish with anything from a bowl of tomato soup to an elegant roast. A side of salad is always good, too. Dig in!

Makes 6 to 8 servings

Ingredients
1 pound elbow macaroni
2 cups milk (whole or 2%, not 1%)
½ cup half-and-half
4 Tablespoons butter, room temperature and cut into pieces
3 Tablespoons flour
2 teaspoons kosher salt
¼ teaspoon freshly ground black pepper
¼ teaspoon dry mustard or cayenne pepper (mustard accentuates the sharpness of the cheese; cayenne adds spiciness)
2 cups sharp white cheddar cheese, grated
½ cup Parmesan cheese, grated
½ cup breadcrumbs

Directions
- Preheat the oven to 375°F.
- In a large pot, cook the macaroni according to the package instructions, just to al dente. Drain and set aside in a large mixing bowl.
- In a saucepan over low heat, heat the milk and cream to near boiling but don't allow to boil. While this is heating up, melt the butter in a high-sided skillet over medium heat. When the butter just starts to bubble, turn the heat down to low and add the flour.
- Stir the butter-flour mixture until combined. Using a whisk, start adding the warm milk and cream, a little at a time. Whisk in each addition of the milk and cream until the combination is smooth. Continue cooking, adding the milk and cream, and whisking constantly to combine the liquid into the sauce.
- When the liquid is incorporated and there are no lumps, continue to cook the sauce on low, stirring with the whisk occasionally, until it thickens, about 3 minutes.

- Add the salt, pepper, and mustard or cayenne and combine thoroughly.
- Stir in the grated cheddar and Parmesan cheeses.
- Pour the cheese sauce over the macaroni and fold it in gently. Transfer the cheesy pasta to a casserole dish. Sprinkle with the breadcrumbs.
- Bake for about 30 minutes until browned on the top and bubbling. Let cool briefly before serving.

More Mac Attacks

There are as many variations of classic macaroni and cheese as there are chefs who make it. While the sauce needs to be made with butter, flour, and milk, the cheeses can be different, and it's not necessary to use just one. Other great choices include Gruyère, smoked gouda, fresh chevre, pecorino Romano, pepper jack, Havarti, even blue cheese. I've enjoyed mac and cheese that also has bacon in it, or diced tomatoes, jalapeños, and even leftover cooked chicken or turkey.

Fresh ingredients make every dish taste better, even if it's as simple as grating your own block of farm-fresh cheese as opposed to buying a prepackaged bag of shredded cheddar.

"Every great chef
needs three things:
good ingredients, the right tools,
and a family to whom
to feed the results."

"The best meal at the end of a long week is hot pizza— with extra pepperoni."

Homemade Pizza

Making pizza at home is fun for everyone, no matter their ages. There's something wonderful about kneading and stretching the dough, and when it's ready for toppings, you can put on whatever you like best. Plan a night with family and friends where you have multiple toppings in bowls and everyone makes individual pizzas. Pizza dough can be made ahead and frozen, too.

Makes 2 standard-sized pizza crusts

Ingredients
3 cups all-purpose flour, plus more as needed
1 packet active dry yeast
2 teaspoons salt
1 cup water
2 Tablespoons olive oil, plus more as needed
Your desired pizza toppings

Directions
- Put the flour in a large mixing bowl. Stir in the yeast and salt.
- Using a wooden spoon to start, add about ¼ cup of the water and stir. Have some paper towels handy and give up the spoon for your hands. Add the water in ¼-cup increments and work the dough until it has formed a slightly sticky ball. If the dough is too dry, add water 1 Tablespoon at a time; if it's too sticky, add flour in 1 Tablespoon increments.
- When you have the right consistency, transfer the dough to a smaller bowl, cover with plastic wrap, and let rise until doubled in size, about 2 hours.
- Working on a clean surface with lightly floured hands, transfer the dough to the counter, reshape it into a ball, and divide it in half. The dough can be refrigerated for several hours, put in plastic bags and frozen for later use, or made into pizzas immediately.
- Working with olive oil on your hands, stretch out a ball with your fingers, make it into as big and thin a circle as you can. Don't use a rolling pin. If you're making individual pizzas, divide the dough into as many as you're making and shape them separately. When the dough is all shaped, brush the baking sheet(s) with olive oil and put the dough on them. Cover with plastic wrap and allow to rest for about 20 minutes.
- Preheat the oven to 500°F.
- "Dress" the pizzas with your desired toppings, working with sauce, then cheese, then other toppings. Pop them in the oven and bake for at least 10 minutes, until crusts are crispy and tops are bubbly.

Peeling Garlic

Fresh garlic is the absolute best choice for flavor. Whether the recipe requires pressing, mincing, or slicing, the skin has to come off the clove. The easiest way to do this is to lay the clove on its side, place the flat blade of your paring knife against it, and press down until it crunches. Slice off the tough top and bottom of the clove, and the skin will peel away.

"From the mouths of moms:
'Try it before you say you don't like it,'
and 'All things in moderation.'"

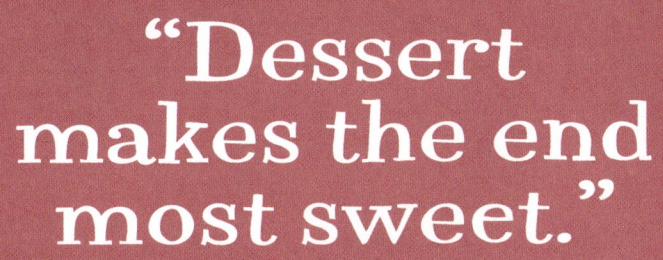

Apple Pie

There's something as enjoyable about making an apple pie as there is about eating one. Picking the apples and helping with the dough are things kids love to be involved in, and when family and friends participate, the pie comes together quickly and easily. This recipe is for a classic pie with a bottom and top crust.

Makes 6 to 8 servings

Crust:
2½ cups flour
½ teaspoon salt
2½ sticks unsalted butter, cut into cubes (the butter should be very cold or even frozen)
4 to 8 Tablespoons cold water

- Combine the flour and salt in a large bowl with a fork.
- If you have a food processor, put the flour-salt mixture in there. Add the cold cubes of butter. If using a food processor, pulse to combine until you have butter pieces about the size of a nickel. If working in the bowl, use a pastry cutter to work the butter into the flour-salt mixture or, best of all, use your fingers (after washing your hands). The dough will form pieces about the size of a nickel.
- Add cold water 2 Tablespoons at a time for the first 4 Tablespoons, and then 1 Tablespoon at a time, pulsing in the food processor or working with the pastry cutter or your hands until the dough holds together and is moist but not wet. Form into two balls.
- Put the balls on a lightly floured surface and flatten them slightly to form disks. Wrap tightly in plastic wrap and refrigerate for at least 1 hour. (The disks can stay in the fridge for up to 2 days.)
- On a lightly floured surface with rolling pin in hand, work the disk evenly, pushing the dough out slowly and evenly. Turn the dough over so it doesn't stick to the surface, making sure there's flour on the top and bottom as you roll.
- When you have a circle that's about 12 inches in diameter, carefully fold it over the rolling pin to center it on the pie plate, and then let the crust drape into the pie plate, pressing down lightly as you place it into the plate.
- Fill the pie before rolling out the second ball of crust that will cover the pie.

Pie:

8 large apples or up to 10 smaller apples, peeled, cored, and cut into eighths
1 lemon
½ cup brown sugar (dark or light)
½ teaspoon cinnamon
⅛ teaspoon nutmeg
¼ teaspoon ground ginger
2 Tablespoons unsalted butter
1 egg

- Preheat the oven to 400°F.
- Rinse apples in a colander, shaking off excess water, and put them in a large bowl.
- Cut the lemon into quarters and remove the seeds. Squeeze the lemon over the slices so they are covered in juice.
- Add the brown sugar, cinnamon, nutmeg, and ginger. Stir the apple pieces to coat with the sugar and spices.
- Carefully put the slices into the pie plate with the bottom crust in it. The apples will form a mound in the pie plate; that's fine. Cut the 2 Tablespoons of butter into slivers and dot them over the apple slices.
- Roll out and drape the top crust over the fruit and pinch together the edges of the top and bottom crusts. Cut 4 slits in the top crust from the middle to halfway down so that the heat can escape while cooking.
- Beat the egg in a small bowl. Use a pastry brush or the back of a fork and brush a film of egg on the top crust. This will form a lovely golden-brown color on the crust.
- Place the pie in the oven and reduce the heat to 375°F. Bake 50–60 minutes, until the crust is golden and the juices are starting to flow. Allow the pie to cool slightly before serving.

Crust Considerations

Don't worry about making the crust by hand—it's really easy and tastes so much better than store-bought. You'll need a rolling pin, for sure, and a 9" pie plate. If you don't want to make the crust, there are multiple options at the store. My order of preference for flavor and freshness is: 1) pie crust mix (you'll still need the rolling pin); 2) crusts that come rolled and in packages of two, which need only to be thawed and draped into the plate and over the fruit; and 3) the premade crusts that are already in the pie plate. This last choice will only work for a classic apple pie if you completely thaw one of the crusts to use it as the top crust.

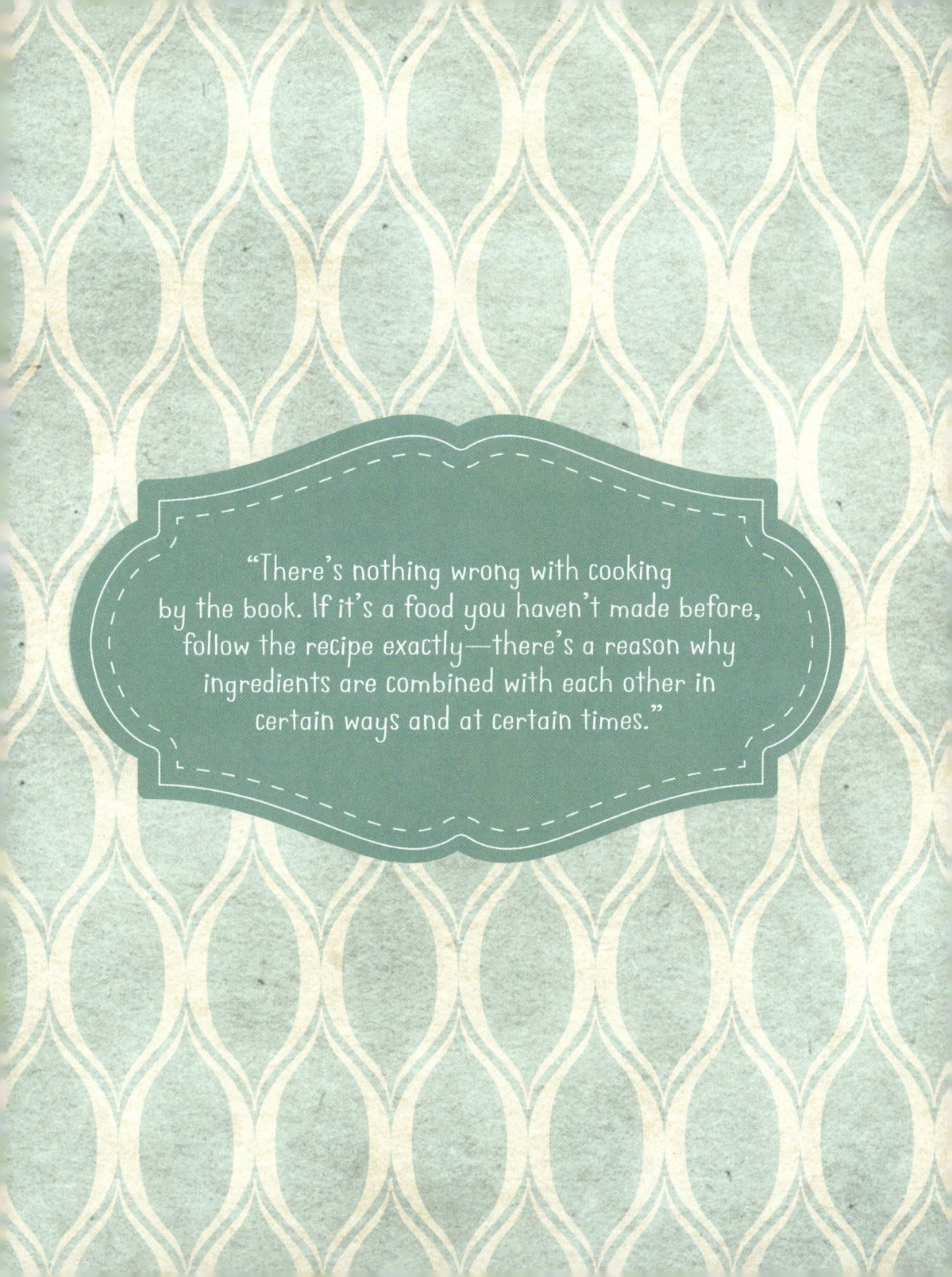

"There's nothing wrong with cooking by the book. If it's a food you haven't made before, follow the recipe exactly—there's a reason why ingredients are combined with each other in certain ways and at certain times."

Chocolate Chip Cookies

I got this recipe off a bag of Gold Medal flour when I was a teenager, and it has stayed with me for many moves. It remains my go-to recipe for the best chocolate chip cookies ever. Thank you, Mary Bartz, who's credited with creating it, and to Gold Medal for making it widely available.

Makes about 3½ dozen cookies

Ingredients
1½ cups (3 sticks) butter or margarine, softened
1¼ cups granulated sugar
1¼ cups packed brown sugar
1 Tablespoon vanilla
2 eggs
4 cups all-purpose flour
2 teaspoons baking soda
1 teaspoon salt
1 package (24 ounces, 4 cups) semisweet chocolate chips

Directions
- Preheat the oven to 350°F.
- In a large bowl, mix the butter, sugars, vanilla, and eggs. Stir in the flour, baking soda, and salt. Stir in the chocolate chips.
- Drop dough by measuring rounded spoonfuls about 2 inches apart onto an ungreased cookie sheet.
- Bake 12–15 minutes, or until light brown. Let cool slightly, remove from cookie sheet. Cool on wire rack.

"The secret to successful cooking is passion."

"THE SMELL OF COOKIES OR BROWNIES BAKING IN THE OVEN BRINGS A FAMILY RUNNING TO THE KITCHEN."

Brownies

It is really easy to make brownies from a mix, and if you use one that's high quality, they can taste darn good. BUT, once you make them from scratch with real chocolate and butter, you will want them that way every time.

Makes 16 squares

Ingredients
8 Tablespoons (1 stick) butter, at room temperature
2 ounces (2 squares) unsweetened baking chocolate
1 teaspoon vanilla
1 cup sugar
½ cup flour
1 teaspoon baking powder
2 eggs

Directions
- Preheat the oven to 350°F. Butter an 8-inch square baking dish.
- Cut the butter into pieces and break up the chocolate squares. Add them to a small microwave-safe bowl. Microwave in intervals of 30 seconds, stirring after each turn, until they are just melted together. Don't overdo it. When melted, add the vanilla.
- In a large bowl, add the sugar, flour, and baking powder. Stir to combine.
- Using a spatula, transfer the chocolate mixture to the large bowl. Stir. Add the eggs and combine thoroughly.
- Put the batter in the square baking dish and bake for 30–45 minutes. The middle should be soft, while a toothpick inserted in it comes out clean. Let cool before serving.

"Colorful frosting flourishes are always worth the extra effort on a special cake, because you do truly eat with your eyes first. Put in the time to make each cake a work of art—you'll be glad you did!"

Cake for Any Occasion

Whether you want to go all-out on a beautiful birthday cake, make a bunch of cupcakes for the kids, or simply have a delicious dessert at the end of the day, this basic vanilla butter cake recipe fits the bill. I often use two layers for a traditional cake and freeze the third round for a later occasion. The cake tastes great frosted in a traditional way, topped with some jam, or simply sprinkled with confectioner's sugar.

Makes 3 9-inch round cakes or nearly 3 dozen cupcakes

Ingredients
3 cups all-purpose flour
4 teaspoons baking powder
½ teaspoon salt
1 cup (2 sticks) butter, softened
2 cups sugar
4 eggs
1 cup milk
1½ teaspoons vanilla

Directions
- Preheat oven to 350°F.
- In a large bowl, add the flour, baking powder, and salt. Stir to combine.
- In another large bowl, cream the butter with the sugar using an electric mixer (or by hand). Add the sugar in ½-cup increments so each addition is thoroughly mixed in. Beat until the mixture is light and fluffy.
- Add one egg at a time, beating until just combined.
- In a small bowl, add the vanilla and milk. Using a spoon (or mixing on low) alternate adding small amounts of the flour mixture and the milk mixture into the butter mixture, until the flour and milk mixtures are used up.
- Spray three round cake pans with nonstick spray, or line cupcake tins with paper or foil cups. Divide the cake batter between the pans or tins, and bake for about 25 minutes for the cakes and 20 minutes for the cupcakes. The top of the cakes should be light golden and spring back at the touch. A toothpick inserted in the center should come out clean.
- Cool the cakes or cupcakes on a wire rack before removing from the pans or tins. Allow to cool completely on the wire racks before frosting with the topping of your choice. If you want to refrigerate or freeze any cakes or cupcakes, once it's completely cooled, wrap it tightly in plastic wrap and refrigerate or freeze.

"Why is it that chocolate cake can almost instantly make you feel better?"

"Rise and shine;
give thanks;
eat mindfully."

**If you have enjoyed this book
or it has touched your life in some way,
we would love to hear from you.**

Please send your comments to:
Hallmark Book Feedback
P.O. Box 419034
Mail Drop 100
Kansas City, MO 64141

Or e-mail us at:
booknotes@hallmark.com